SHOOTING FOR THE MOON

Love Poems from First Date to Forever

D. Lisette

Luna Publishing LLC

ISBN 979-8-218-93376-0 (Paperback Edition)

Editing by Luna Publishing, LLC
Front cover by D. Lisette
Book design by D. Lisette

Printed and bound in the United States of America
First Printing June 2026

Published by Luna Publishing, LLC
Contact us at admin@lunapublishingllc.com

Dedicated to the man who lights up my life and always knows how to make me smile.

-D. Lisette

PREFACE

These poems started seven years ago in a dorm room. They were intended for an audience of one.

My husband and I started dating in 2019, and what a rollercoaster it was. At our Christian university, it felt like God had aligned the stars for us to meet. In 2021, we joyfully tied the knot. These poems are my raw and unfiltered thoughts during our dating, engaged, and married years.

All in seven years, we have gone through academic stress, the prime of our college days, the grief of losing a parent, the joys of wedding planning, the unknowns of a relationship, the healing of trauma, the security of marriage, and the birth of our first child. Through it all, my sentiments of love and devotion from the very beginning have remained the same.

The title was inspired by my husband's last name—our last name—and it is a fun play on that common quote. I've always been an overachiever, so I like the idea of having actually hit my target—the moon—instead of just the stars.

I hope readers find the pure and honest truths of Christian love in these poems. Keeping ourselves for marriage was not the easy road, but it was worth it. As the poems are chronological to when they were written, you'll be able to see the struggle and the eventual reward of being obedient to Christ in all aspects of our lives, especially when it comes to romantic relationships.

May you find encouragement for your own love story in these pages.

SHOOTING FOR THE MOON

12.2018

Roses are red,
Violets are blue,
I can’t wait
To see you.
Daisies are yellow;
You’re a nice fellow.
My head swirls
With thoughts of you
Every time
My head hits the pillow.

SHOOTING FOR THE MOON

01.12.2019

My thoughts sound better on paper
Than they do coming from my mouth,
So trust that when I give you a note,
It has been painstakingly thought out.
Read what it says carefully
Because it’s my heart on the page;
I do better on paper
Than I do on a stage.
Hopefully one day I will articulate out loud
All the things my heart feels when it pounds,
But for now I have a pen and a page,
And I think
“You make me feel safe and so very brave.
You are wonderful in so many ways”
Is what I’m trying to say.

SHOOTING FOR THE MOON

01.17.2019

We stare at each other,
Saying nothing, doing nothing,
But it feels like everything;
It is everything
Because
You make hours feel like minutes,
And each minute lasts an hour.
I can't comprehend how this works,
But keep doing it;
I never want it to end.

01.18.2019

Good night, good night,
Sweet dreams,
And sleep tight.
Dream and dream
With all your might;
I'll see you again
When the sun shines bright.

SHOOTING FOR THE MOON

01.25.2019

I think it’s beautiful
That you, the moon,
And me, the sun,
Happened to see each other in the sky.
You said, “What a beautiful day,”
And I thought, “What a beautiful night.”
We rise and fall with the times;
We keep each other balanced and right,
And every time you say “Good morning”
I make sure to say a “Good night.”

01.27.2019 #1

When you kissed me a few nights ago,
It ignited a fire in my chest
And stole my breath.
So I hope you know
I keep my promises
With every ounce of me.
Yes, I keep them with all my depth.
I have promised
To always encourage you,
Be there for you, be honest with you,
And that you can trust me too.
I have yet to show you
Even a little of my depth,
But with patience
And baby steps,
You'll be the one
To get the furthest yet;
I want you to be
The one
To get the furthest.
Don't give up on me
Because I, too, don't give up easily.

01.27.2019 #2

Kiss me in the dark
Under all the stars
When the moon is shining bright—
Our only source of light.
Kiss me softly;
Kiss me slow,
But kiss me just enough
To remind me
You'll never let me go.
Hold me tight
With your gentle might,
And please never ever leave my side.

01.31.2019

Colorblind boy:
Curly hair in a whirl.
He smiles like vanilla
And talks like chocolate—
I may have painter's hands,
But he has painted my heart
Colors I never knew existed.
This colorblind boy
Reviving my colorblind heart.

SHOOTING FOR THE MOON

02.03.2019

When I look into your eyes, I see the sky.
I count the stars inside your head;
I get lost in the galaxy of your depth.
There may be black holes
From your past
Where your heart has bled,
But all I see is light instead.
All I see is light instead.

02.05.2019

When I'm tired,
I just want to fall into your arms,
Rest my head on your shoulder,
And forget the world exists.
I want to bask in your warmth
And feel the heartbeat in your chest.
I am comforted by your presence
Just knowing you are there.
I feel safe
And forget all my cares.

SHOOTING FOR THE MOON

02.07.2019

Do not only kiss my lips;
Kiss my mind.
Kiss it with questions
That leave me pondering
Long after the conversation has ended.
Kiss my heart
With yours
When you pull me into your embrace,
And kiss my soul
With your eyes—
That passionate fiery gaze.

02.08.2019

I could write a book,
Fill every page
Of all the things
I want to say.
It would be full of my heart,
Full of you.
Full of thoughts
Prayers and dreams—
Full of the time
I spend
Thinking of
You.

SHOOTING FOR THE MOON

02.09.2019

I know you feel like
The walls are closing in.
There’s too much going on;
Your strength is wearing thin,
But keep on going.
Keep on growing.
Don’t let the system steal
Your joy of learning.
When the darkness is all around,
Remember that with God,
Light is always found.

02.12.2019

In the worlds inside my mind
Is where I hide,
And there is where
I could only ever confide.
But then you came,
You came into my life.
Took my hand by your side,
Brought me along,
And welcomed me into your life.
I’m surprised,
And I’m grateful to say
I want to be with you
And know you
More and more
Everyday.

02.13.2019

You’re the only man my lips have ever touched,
And that’s why I value each kiss so much.
Maybe that’s why one is never enough.

02.14.2019

"You hold my heart.
Don't let it shatter—
Please don't let it break"
Is something I thought
I would only hear myself say.
But that's what you said to me,
And for some reason that was surprising.
So I will hold your heart
The best I know how,
But please forgive me
If I stumble somehow.
I've never held
Someone else's heart before;
I'm afraid I'll let you down.
I don't want it to shatter;
I don't want it to break
Because believe me when I say,
"You are holding my heart
In the same way."

SHOOTING FOR THE MOON

02.16.2019

Para mi Príncipe de la Luna:

Cuando la Princesa del Sol
Descendió su cabeza para descansar,
El Príncipe de la Luna
Levantó la suya
Y la llenó con esperanzas de verla,
Completamente radiante y cegadora.
Antes de que su última luz se fuera,
Ella lo besó con uno de sus
Rayos dorados persistentes;
Lo dejó con un suave resplandor,
El cual duró toda la noche
E ilumino las estrellas.

As the Sun Princess
Descended to rest her head,
The Moon Prince
Lifted his
And filled it with hopes of seeing her
Full, blinding radiance.
Before the last of her light was gone,
She kissed him with one of her
Lingering golden rays;
It left him with a gentle glow
That lasted the night
And illuminated the stars.

-La Princesa del Sol

02.23.2019 #1

Tangerines and pineapples,
Pianos and drums,
My silence, his hum—
A beautifully strange love.

SHOOTING FOR THE MOON

02.23.2019 #2

I've seen you walk around
With the fears in your head.
I've seen the hurt in your eyes
As you remember times
When your heart was mislead.
You have shown me your heavy heart,
So let me hold it;
I want to hold you
And be the one you come to
When your soul feels dark,
Or when your heart is blue,
When your knuckles are bruised,
When you've fought too long
And just need to be held.
I want to be the one
To help break the spell
Of all the fears you hide—
Killing you slowly—
Killing you inside.
Give them to God,
Then come to me.
I will always be here for you:
Comforting,
Comforting.

02.23.2019 #3

I have universes inside my mind.
Universes I want to show you,
Galaxies of everything I am.
There are things I want to do,
A lifetime of things to say.
But sometimes I can't;
I, myself, get in the way.
It's just that my words
Seem to get lost in the stars,
Or maybe they drown in black holes,
Or maybe they get stuck orbiting
The planet of my brain.
I hope you know
You have my permission
To get closer,
To look further inside.
I want to be known;
I don't want to hide.
And I'm sorry if it seems
That I play hide and seek
With my heart.
It's just that I've hidden it so, so
Far down in me
That sometimes I forget
I am the one with the key.
There are things I'm still unlocking,
So please be patient with me,
And don't give up on me
Because for you I want to bloom.
I want to bloom
Beautifully.

SHOOTING FOR THE MOON

02.26.2019

You love me as LOUDLY
As neon yellow: your favorite color.
It's as passionate and bright as the sun.
It's electric; it glows
Like the neon yellow only your eyes know.
I love you as softly
As emerald green: my favorite color.
It is as deep and constant as a drum.
It is steadfast; it grows
Like the emerald green only my heart knows.

02.28.2019

Pure love:
I love you in the purest ways.
I love seeing that smile on your face,
Or when you laugh and it reaches your eyes,
And when you melt me with hugs.
I love every tear your eyes hide,
And when you're sad I feel it too.
I love you in the purest ways;
I love all the silly things you say
And all the small things you do.
When you tell me "It will be ok,"
I find myself believing you.
I want you to be nothing but happy,
And I want to see your wildest dreams
Come true.
Truly it is true!
I love you in the purest ways;
I really do.

SHOOTING FOR THE MOON

03.02.2019

I woke up
With a lin g er i n g taste
From the night before:
The flavor of you sat
On my lips,
And if someone got too close,
They might infer I was hungover
From your kisses.
I have never been drunk before,
But the taste of your lips was enough
To show me what it might be like.

SHOOTING FOR THE MOON

03.04.2019

Sometimes I am a little afraid
To want you completely,
To admit you're what
My heart craves.
And who knows,
Maybe sometimes you feel that way too.
But I want you to know
I find it brave of us
To be
Here
Both sitting
Together
Believing our story could be
Any different
When so many have failed.
Both sitting
Together
Smiling
In the face of fear.

SHOOTING FOR THE MOON

03.07.2019

I love you because you are simply you.
I love you because you are free.
I love you because you speak boldly,
And because you are everything
I've never been able to be.
I love you because it makes me want to be
Everything that I can be.
I want to be more of me for you,
And that's what I think is
Lovely about us.
We choose to see stars
In each other's dust.

03.09.2019

I like the hum my heart makes
When it’s with you:
A tune like a lullaby,
A lullaby that wakes up my hopes
And puts to sleep my fears.
A minor melancholy lullaby
Singing for what will be
But isn’t yet.
A lullaby that ends with a major sound
Because it hopes and dreams and believes
It will keep the love it has found.

SHOOTING FOR THE MOON

03.12.2019

Lilac skies can’t compare to your eyes
When you stare into mine.
They erase all space and time;
Then our heartbeats collide.
The supernova of your love
Is something I couldn’t have dreamed of.
Pupils like black holes,
I fall into you.
I drown in the sea of stars
Which is your heart.
I feel like an astronaut on the moon.
The moon so bright and true!
So bright, so you.

03.16.2019 #1

I often wonder
What it will look like
In the future
With you by my side,
With me by yours.
I wonder what we will be
Or who we will become.
It’s not hard to imagine,
And maybe that’s the part
I find amazing:
That this could be real
And not just a dream.

03.16.2019 #2

You have
Lollipop lips—
The only ones I want to kiss,
Subtly strong hands of
Coffee-colored skin
Pulling me in,
And eyes like chocolate—
A river I want to drown in.

03.16.2019 #3

And sometimes
I still try to figure out
How you stole my heart—
How you came in so suddenly,
So silently yet in
Complete visibility.
I watched it unfold
Before my very eyes.
You stole my heart,
And I didn’t even try to stop you.
I didn’t want to stop you,
And I hope you find it
As amazing as I do;
Yes, you may have stolen my heart,
But I also gave it to you.

SHOOTING FOR THE MOON

03.21.2019 #1

You mean
Everything
To me,
And there's no sea too deep,
No galaxy so vast
That could get me to
Release you from my grasp.
You are mine;
I've firmly made that decision
In my heart
And in my mind.

03.21.2019 #2

Ours is a childlike love—
Lost in the wonder of each other,
Playful and honest.
Ours is a mature and realistic love—
Holding on to one another,
Deciding to love each other.
As iron sharpens iron,
So one person sharpens another.
We have both been
Forged in the fire
So that it turns into a holy passion
For God who calls us higher.

SHOOTING FOR THE MOON

03.22.2019

There's something so pure
About just resting my head on your shoulder,
About being held in your arms when I'm sleepy.
I simply desire
To slip into slumber
With my face nestled
Between your chest and your neck.
I want to hear your heartbeat
Thundering under
The weight of my head;
I want to dream at the pace
Of the rise and fall of your breath.

03.29.2019

As I slip off to slumber,
I think of you.
I think of all the things
We will say and do.
There are many things to tell you,
So many things to hear,
And that's why I hold you close;
That's why I call you dear.

SHOOTING FOR THE MOON

04.03.2019

I hope it doesn't seem
As if I say
"I love you" too much
Because I feel like
I never say it enough.
I find it easy to love you;
It just
   s
    p
      i
          l
              l
                s right out,
Right from my heart
To the front of my mouth.
I hope it never becomes
Casual to your attentive ears
Because when I say it,
It's never out of habit—
It's with a depth
You could drown in
And so much weight
You could grab it.

SHOOTING FOR THE MOON

04.04.2019

You're going to do amazing things, babe;
I already know
Because people like you
Don't take "no" for an answer,
And up is the only way to go.
So when the road seems long
And things start to get tough,
Remember I'm here:
I'll be lifting you up.

04.07.2019 #1

Strong tree roots
Are the veins of your hand—
The course of your blood
Running along the frame
Of your body,
Which is its land.

04.07.2019 #2

There are things I love,
And some I cannot live without:
The way a sunset looks with clouds in the sky,
Warm blankets and snuggles on a rainy day,
Deep long conversations that leave me bare,
And your loving arms and eyes filled with care.

SHOOTING FOR THE MOON

04.11.2019

I wish I could
Hug all your worries away
And kiss all your stresses goodbye;
I want to hold you
Until the peace of mind returns,
And I want to
Hold you so close
That you can feel
The fire in my heart
As it burns.

SHOOTING FOR THE MOON

04.12.2019

Moments with you
Go by too quickly,
Gone in a flash.
I think of all the times
We've spent together
In these months past,
And all I know is that
I love being with you;
I love you.
And with you I want
To breakthrough
As the ones who
Break the chain,
Change the cycle,
Heal the pain,
And change the game.
Because despite our parents' pasts,
I like to believe our love is one
That will last.

SHOOTING FOR THE MOON

04.16.2019

She fell in love with the moon,
For his soft light
Illuminated beautiful things that
Could not have been seen
Except when in contrast with
The vast darkness.
Like the way she hummed to herself
In the night,
Or the way her heart jumped
When caught in his sight.

04.19.2019

Promise me
You can protect me from yourself—
From the darkness within—
When the light gets dull,
When breath gets thin.

Can we protect each other
From ourselves?
From the sinful flesh within—
That monster inside,
The one we all starve,
The one we all hide,
Praying it never comes back
To life?

04.22.2019

The moments I love the most
Are not the ones you'd think.
I love the small things you do
And things you say
That make me think—
The quiet, small,
And sometimes routine
Things we do.
It's those simple moments
When I remember why
I love you.

SHOOTING FOR THE MOON

04.25.2019

The other day I was looking at a picture of us;
It was a lovely picture
When we were young and full of life.
As I looked, I saw a flash of us through time.
I blinked at the picture and looked again.
We were old together—
Hand in hand,
Grey hair and wrinkly—
But on your face, the same youthful smile:
Your eyes still shining brightly
And in my heart the deepest love
Like a fire inside me.

SHOOTING FOR THE MOON

05.01.2019

It’s perplexing how,
At the same time,
You can be
The wildest adventure
And a peaceful song—
How you make me feel
Daring
But also safe in your arms.
I’ll admit
I was afraid,
At the start of it,
To fall into this thing called “love,”
But I took the leap
Despite the fear—
Opened my heart,
Let you near.
While falling
I had a thought:
Will he love me?
Will he not?
I fell and fell,
And fear fell too.
You caught me,
But the fear you threw.

05.09.2019

I want to immortalize you
With my words
And construct phrases
Depicting your passion
For life, for love, and for God.
When the flames seem to fade,
I want you to be able
To look back, read, and remember
What it was like to be on
Fire.
When the rain comes,
I hope you find it within yourself
To burn all the
Brighter.

SHOOTING FOR THE MOON

05.13.2019

A yearning has gripped my heart
Since last we pulled our lips apart
And I watched the wheels start;
We'll see each other soon
After many more moons—
If only you knew
How much I miss you:
I kiss the air
And tell the wind
To carry it to you,
But we'll see each other soon
Before the fade of summer's bloom.

SHOOTING FOR THE MOON

05.14.2019

A pair of lips is only
Half a heart,
So when we put ours together,
I can feel my life begin to start.
Where the tiny freckle on mine
Meets the smooth dip in yours—
Of this I have never been more sure:
That the dip of your lip was
Made perfectly for my lips to fit,
And the freckle on mine
Was made to plot constellations
On your smile line.

SHOOTING FOR THE MOON

05.17.2019

Oh, how little you know
Of how cold my heart had become—
Locked behind walls,
Never to see the sun.
All warmth and love was
But a facade to cover what was within
Because I never trusted anyone enough
To let them in.
Frozen by fear,
Frozen in ice,
But then I saw your eyes,
And they looked so warm;
They looked so kind.
You got closer and closer
Until you could no more,
And I found myself
Giving you permission
To bust down the door.
But instead of brute force
You slowly came in
Warming my heart
With everything you did.
Little by little
The walls of ice melted away,
And you started a fire in my heart
With your passionate gaze.
Sometimes I pushed back
Here and there,
Worrying, wondering,
Why you even cared.
A few times I burned
rom feeling your wrath
But decided to cool you off
And bring you back.
Even you have been stung
By my silence

And the ice in my eyes,
But your loving fire grew brighter
Much to my surprise.
So I guess that's just what happens
When ice falls in love with fire
And when fire falls in love with ice.

SHOOTING FOR THE MOON

05.26.2019

I can’t feel you anymore;
We feel so far apart.
I search for you in my heart,
But I find myself in the dark:
To hear your voice say, “I love you,”
To feel your warmth, and to hug you.
I hate this distance between
Everything we hope and dream.
This time for which we have been apart
Is starting to tear up my heart.
Through distance and through unknowns,
Please remind me you’ll never let go
And that your love,
Our love,
Will continue to grow.

SHOOTING FOR THE MOON

05.27.2019

Young warrior,
Do not give up in this war:
For you may feel that darkness surrounds you,
But Jesus is at the door.
Angels surround you,
And it's you they fight for.
It's not about pushing darkness out
As much as it is letting the Light in,
And for every sin,
There is also forgiveness
And a chance to start again.
So remember, my love,
To take a deep breath,
And let Jesus lead you to the win.

SHOOTING FOR THE MOON

06.03.2019

I could write all the poems,
But it would never be enough
Because no combination of words
Could ever fully describe
This amazingly beautiful
Love.

06.12.2019

The protector and the poet:
You fight in physicality
For us
While I wield with words
Against enemies.
You protect my body,
My voice;
I soothe you with my phrases.
Our lips entwined
Promising protection, provision,
And prayer—
And poetry and purity
With every peck,
With every pulse of our hearts.
A wholesomeness
Hanging on words constructed
By hands of love holding a pen.
Protect my heart
So that I may turn us into art.

SHOOTING FOR THE MOON

06.17.2019

How can two parts make a whole?
How can two pieces broken from
Something that used to be whole
Come together
And ever make anything different?
How can it make anything stronger
Than the material it was broken from?
Does breaking one thing
To build another
Make the new stronger?
I am uncertain,
But maybe that's why our families
Were broken in two—
So that our hearts would break
At the exact shape
To fit the other's.

06.26.2019

So**m**e say the most mean**i**ngful poem
Is a name,
But really, I think the phrase
"I miss you"
Is the most meaningful
Be**c**ause it tells of **h**ow
One he**a**rt
Has been so chang**e**d,
So **l**oved,
So connected to another's
That physical distance
Creates a physica**l**
H**u**rt—
An emptiness
Which cannot be cured
Until both hearts
Are together again—
An i**n**expressible longing
Which can only be expressed
In **a** way that conveys
Incompleteness.

SHOOTING FOR THE MOON

06.28.2019

You will have to be patient with me,
For sometimes I walk in contradiction.
Not that I am two-faced
Or of a double mind, but
It's often that I am fighting with who I am
And who I am trying to be.
It's true, sometimes I can have
A cold kindness,
A sad smile,
A gentle wrath,
Or a cautious boldness;
I don't see eye to eye,
And sometimes the contradictions
Get the best of me.
Please don't give up on me
Through my controlled insanity,
For you have the ability to make
My heart stop or beat.
Yes, keep doing what you're doing
Because your love makes me want
To keep counteracting
The contradictions within me.

07.08.2019 #1

You are vermillion—
Sweet and sour soup,
The only one I want to spoon.

07.08.2019 #2

Tickle me,
Or make me laugh until I can't breathe.
Then pull me close
And steal what remaining breath I may have
With a long firm kiss.

07.12.2019 #1

I am a four page love letter
In a world of quick texts:
Not everyone wants to take the time
To read.
But oh, for the one who does!
I am a cup of strong black coffee
In a world of watered down dreams:
Not everyone wants a taste of my life.
But oh, for the one who does!
When the pages seem to go on,
And as the coffee gets stronger,
Don't for a moment imagine
That I won't want you any longer;
Nothing could be farther
From the truth.
This simple love poem
Is the proof.

07.12.2019 #2

I realized how
Entangled
My heart was with yours
When I saw your sad eyes
And prayed to God
That I could be the one to comfort them.
I realized when I realized
I was not afraid to feel your feelings
As my own
Because I'd rather hurt with you
Than for you to hold it alone.

SHOOTING FOR THE MOON

07.17.2019

It all feels so heavy:
The hurt,
The pain,
The sin,
The shame.
It makes this love feel like a game,
And if it doesn't stop then I'll go insane.
We promised each other purity,
But purity is a fight
Which the devil tries to corrupt
Through carefully constructed lies.
Speaking the truth will set us free
And take away our misery.
Crucify the lies
Before they plant seeds in your mind.
Have no mercy on darkness or sin;
Do not make peace
With what causes chaos.
Fight against it with all the strength
Of the angels surrounding you,
Our forefathers running before you,
And the Holy Spirit within you.
The enemy would love nothing more
Than to end a powerful partnership
Before it knocks down his walls
And deceptive doors.
Our purity is power,
And that's why we must battle
For the godly love
To which we profess
Until we have walked down that aisle—
You in a suit
And me in a pure white dress.

07.29.2019 #1

I can't wait to lay by your side,
To roll over in the middle of the night
And feel you by my side
Because when the monsters come
I need to know
You will hold me tight.
Although I'm brave,
And though I can fight,
Sometimes I just need
The extra reminder
That everything
Will be alright.

07.29.2019 #2

I want to write you a poem,
But I don't know if it would be very good.
I want to write you a poem;
I really wish I could.
The words aren't coming—
Darkness is a block to my brain.
I want to write you a poem,
But lately my mind
Just hasn't been the same.
For a writer that's frustrating,
And it makes me want to go insane
Because I want to tell you
How much I love you
With every fancy phrase.
My heart keeps shouting
"Love!" and "Freedom!",
But my mind slips down the steps of pain.
I want to write you a poem,
But I'll just have to wait
Until my mind has a heart
And my heart has a brain.

SHOOTING FOR THE MOON

08.02.2019

I see the depth of your heart,
The fire in your eyes,
And the injustice that tears you apart.
I see the depth of your heart
And blood boil in your veins;
You want to end any pain
Before it even starts.
That's the part of Jesus in you I can see:
A superhero wanting to set people free,
And if there's any part of Him in me,
It's compassion and understanding.
Any response of concern
Was from a source of deep love—
Concern for your heart and that
Unfairness unchecked might tear it apart.
I've seen what it can do,
And my display of concern
Over immediate understanding
Was the result of me
Just wanting to protect you.
I hope you never doubt
How deep my love is for you.
It may not seem like I do,
But please believe me, babe,
I understand you.

SHOOTING FOR THE MOON

08.04.2019

My hands,
You thought they were painted
And asked why they were red.
Blind to their bumps, yes,
The color caught your attention instead.
You didn’t see the decay on my skin;
You saw the artist and painter within.
You didn’t see a mess;
You saw a maker.
You saw them at a glance
But even seeing them clearly
Decided they were hands
You wanted to grasp.
So hold them tight when they shake,
When they want to destroy
Instead of create,
For when you hold them close
You keep me safe.
Kiss them,
And whisper purpose with your lips;
Set them on fire
With the will to create.

SHOOTING FOR THE MOON

08.05.2019

Would you compare me to a summer's day—
How I blaze with fire,
Ready for what comes my way?
Or would you liken me to soft falling snow—
Blowing wherever the wind goes?
Or maybe you think
I am like lightning and rain:
Capable of watering others,
Using everything I have
To light up their world for one moment
But left with nothing for myself.
If one thing is for certain,
I would compare you
To an early Sunday morning:
Full of forgiveness, remnants of soft dreams,
White sheets, and full of belief.

SHOOTING FOR THE MOON

08.08.2019

I am a flower, and your words are water.
My pedals will bloom or close
At the flow of your tone.
Let love and encouragement
Drip from your lips:
Be careful what you say,
For poisonous words will wilt me away.

I am a song, and you are the singer.
Your tone sets the tune
We will dance to.
Learn to breathe
In the right timing,
And only then will our sound
Echo in the air.

I am a flower;
I am a song.
You are the water;
You are strong.
You are the singer:
It's my hum
Your lips are hooked on.

SHOOTING FOR THE MOON

08.15.2019

Salty lips
From the summer heat
Tickles my tongue
As hand and sweaty back meet.
You whispered you missed me,
So I say, "then never leave."

Your lips tasted like flowers
As if you had sipped my perfume
In the late night humidity
Under a waxing moon.
Kisses are promises
Making my lungs contract faster.
When I kiss you, I remind myself:
"I am safe. I am loved.
My mind is not a disaster."

SHOOTING FOR THE MOON

08.26.2019

You once said I was glass,
And I think that it is true,
For glass is formed through fire,
And heat gives it its hue.
It breaks under too much pressure
But withstands extreme temperature.
Glass absorbs and reflects
The Light that is around,
And in its scratches or cracks
Beauty can be found.
Cracks came from when I had been dropped
By my own hands or another's—
Still learning to rest
In the loving arms of the Father.
And yes, we've had circumstances
That aren't ideal,
But if I'm glass,
Then that makes you steel.
We are strong and stubborn.
We are spearheads for what God wants to do.
We are spearheads for what He wants to use us
To pierce through.

SHOOTING FOR THE MOON

09.03.2019

We had not looked at each other
For what seemed like an eternity.
Blinded by hurt
With pain as our enemy,
But finally we blinked.
We could see clearly,
And you said my eyes were green.
But what did you mean?
Green like the grass
Or like the water in the sea?
Was it dark and brooding
Like moss in a stream?
Or was it light and pale
Like glass on the street?
My dear colorblind boy,
Your eyes must see a specific beauty,
For my eyes look brown to me.

SHOOTING FOR THE MOON

09.13.2019

I love your hands on my body
Even when they just rest on my leg.
I love how they are soft and firm,
And when you play piano, they shake.
I love your hands in my hair
And how you stroke my face;
You know how to touch me
In all the right ways.
You have musician's hands,
So of course they would move along
The instrument of my body
With purpose, passion, and playfulness
To illicit joyful noises
And sounds of praise.
Contrary to what society may teach,
A touch doesn't have to be a sexual thing
For it to make my body sing.
Understanding this simple truth
Is a facet of your love
You continue to prove.

SHOOTING FOR THE MOON

09.17.2019

You've finally found a flow,
And now things feel slow.
Everything is kinda boring,
So you sigh and say,
"Here we go."
I just want to remind you,
And I hope you know,
Anything I do with you
Or anywhere we go
Is the most exciting thing
My heart has ever known.
Find joy in the mundane.
Find peace at this pace,
For God will give you the grace
To run this race.
Grab my hand
And let's go
On this adventure of unknowns,
So take a deep breath because
"Here we go!"

SHOOTING FOR THE MOON

09.27.2019

Sometimes I'm convinced that
You love me more than I love myself.
You say I am worthy of everything,
So why do I find it so hard
To ask for help?
You say I am loved, beautiful, and free,
So why do I feel like
I'm trapped in a hazy dream?
It's frustrating because I can't wake up.
The nightmare is reality,
But you say I light up your world—
The noise around you grows faint.
I'm good at bringing joy to others,
But none for myself do I take.
So just kiss me,
And remind me why it's good to be alive.
Just kiss me and kiss me
Until I no longer feel dead inside.
Hold me tighter
When I'm about to break.
Never leave my side:
Remind me I am loved.
Remind me I am safe.
Remind me I am brave.

SHOOTING FOR THE MOON

10.14.2019

You look dashing
In dimly lit rooms—
How the soft light
Cascades across your body
Creating shadows around
The hills and valleys
Of your face,
Wrapping itself around
The definition
Of your muscles,
And casting mystery
On your torso.
It's a dull glow
On your dark skin—
An alluring effect
That draws me in.

10.22.2019

We fell in love
In winter
Under the light of the full moon's glow.
We fell in love
In winter
After winter's first snow.
We fell in love in winter,
A time when things no longer grow,
Yet our love grew
In the winter,
And this only do I know:
That I will love you
In every season,
And I'm never letting go.

SHOOTING FOR THE MOON

11.11.2019

Homecoming was like a dream,
And you made me feel like a queen.
I forget about my cares
When you pull me in
And we dance to
The rhythm of our heart beats.
To be the one
You chose to dance with
In a crowded room,
It made me feel like the
Prettiest flower in bloom.
To kiss you in
The thick of the heat,
While people are bouncing
To the boom of the beat,
Made time stand still.
With everyone singing in thrill,
With the chaos of celebration around,
You only have my eyes found:
It's just you and me in this room now.
No matter how we may have ended the night,
I choose to only remember us dancing
Close together
Gazing into each other's eyes.

11.15.2019

A girlfriend’s prayer:

May Your voice be magnified
In his life, Lord,
And may I only speak
Your wise words
When he feels like
He’s lost his way.
Shout louder than the insecurities
Pounding his brain,
And may only Your Truth remain:
That he was made to worship You
Through joy and through pain.
Remind him You’re there
And You’re not playing games,
And when he feels lost,
Or all seems hopeless,
Remind him that
It’s his voice you want to use
To break through the darkness.
His voice is a light,
A beacon for the lost like him.
Give him hope
So that his dreams
Would not be placed
On the shelf.
In Jesus’ name,
Amen.

SHOOTING FOR THE MOON

11.29.2019

I am thankful
For your loyalty
And how you run to me
When I am deeply
Lost in the sea of sadness
That sometimes overtakes me.
I am grateful for how
You love me on the good days,
The bad, and everything in between.
I thank God for you
In my thoughts throughout the day,
And I hope it shows in my actions
And encouragement of you everyday.
I am thankful for your laugh,
Your curly hair, and your handsome smile;
I am grateful to be the one
Who has the power
To bring your smile back
When it has been gone for a while.
I am honored to be your friend
And faithful love—
To be the one I get to show
The love of Christ to—
Because there's no one else
I would rather it be.
So what I'm trying to say
Is Happy Thanksgiving,
And I love this life
That we are living.

SHOOTING FOR THE MOON

12.07.2019

I have tree eyes:
Deep, dark, and wise—
Brown with a green hue
When the sunlight hits them just right,
According to you.
Many say the eyes
Are a window to the soul,
But for you
My eyes are vines
Down which you climb
To reach my roots.
When you reach the bottom,
I hope you find the truth.
The truth that I have
Always
Rooted for you,
Believed in you,
And will
Always
Love you.

12.13.2019

I love you more than Christmas lights,
Much to my surprise.
I love you more than Christmas lights;
You have a different type of sparkle
In your eyes.
I love you more than Christmas lights—
Surely it’s no surprise.
I love you more than Christmas lights,
And you light up my life.

12.19.2019

I love you babiiiii
You are so snugglyyyyyy
I love you more than treeeeeee
You are precious to meeeee

SHOOTING FOR THE MOON

12.29.2019

I really want to kiss you.
Have I mentioned I miss you?
I want to breathe you in;
I want to be closer than your skin.
I want to hold you;
I want to be held.
I want to be taken from this place;
I want my heart to melt.

SHOOTING FOR THE MOON

03.23.2020

Burnt boy, burnt boy
Feeling like a dirty toy.
So scared and so bruised—
Feeling so used.
Can anybody see your pain?
People like to think,
"No tears? No shame."
So forgive me for hurting you;
Please believe I never intended to.
And from your past,
You probably have more burnt spots than I do.
Burnt boy, burnt boy,
You made me your mirror,
But still, you cannot see any clearer.
A dirty rendition of His image—
Bare as bone
Before the throne.
You just want to find this place
Called "Whole."

SHOOTING FOR THE MOON

04.04.2020

I wish I could take away all your grief,
And if we lived together,
I would tell you to stay in bed
While I make you some tea.
I wish I could give you some relief
And help you carry this sadness
All too deep and too heavy.

I wish I could change your belief
That you can't let your guard down.
I would hate to see you drown,
But maybe this process is part of fixing your crown
From all the times it's fallen down.
Every new king mourns the loss of his father
Although it is the loss
That takes the kingdom even farther.
Surely, victory will come from this misery,
And a sense of duty to carry on the legacy.
So carry on the legacy, take it to the heights.
Because then we'll look back and say,
"They're right, legends never die."

SHOOTING FOR THE MOON

05.08.2020

His skin was made of gold.
You could see it in the sun's light—
Glistening in his cheeks,
Sparkling in his eyes.
Had a heart of gold too;
It's no surprise.
Raven ringlet curls
In contrast with his
Golden caramel skin.
With eyes so deep
And smile so bright,
Can't help but desire his lips on my body tonight;
Can't help but desire his arms to hold me tight.

SHOOTING FOR THE MOON

05.29.2020

I miss those eyes,
Communicating with words
The dictionary doesn’t know.
I miss holding those hands,
Twisting together
Like tree roots still to grow.
I miss those lips;
I miss them more than you know.
Hold my hips, and pull me close.
Kiss me firmly,
But kiss me slow.
I want to gaze into your eyes.
I want you to know
That I am yours
And yours alone.

06.19.2020

Tonight:

I just want the nights of us laughing at each other at two in the morning. I want to laugh with you more.

I want the moments of us running out into the rain and splashing in puddles together.

I want you to live in the same space as me. I even want the opportunity to get tired of you being in the same space as me all the time.

I want the nights when we run away to IHOP and just are free for a moment—outside of the constraints and responsibilities of the day.

I want the snuggles at night with no obligation to be anywhere else, with no obligation to "watch" ourselves.

I want whimsy and spontaneity. Dullness weighs down on me.

I want to sit on the sidewalk with you and let others stare at us as they walk by.

I want our love to never die.

I want midnight piano serenades and early morning ice cream sundaes.

I want to dance with you in the parking lot under the stars.

I want to do it all with you. I want all of you. I just want you.

SHOOTING FOR THE MOON

I want to live my life with you to the fullest. The dullness weighs down on me.

And I just want to be free.

I just want to love you freely.

SHOOTING FOR THE MOON

06.21.2020

It happened too fast,
So you tried to shove it past.
No flowers were given.
All the words you would have said
Now lie underground, hidden.
Your golden status
Reduced to feelings of ashes
And with it all your passions.
It's hard when
The world doesn't even let you choose
To go and see the place where he lay—
Where your heart currently lies, too.
You want to be brave.
You want to scream the things
You wanted to say.
Golden boy, golden boy,
His light still shines on you.
Stay gold for Him, and him,
And for me too.
I love you.

07.20.2020

You make me feel like the color green:
Vibrant and bright,
Beautiful and serene.
You make me feel like the color red:
Bursting with love,
And so many wonderful thoughts
Fill my head.
So when you're missing a hue,
Here's what you should do:
Look at me,
And I'll help you see them,
I'll help you feel them too.

08.31.2020

It's raining,
And I love you.
It's raining,
And all I can think of is you—
Maybe because you always
Make my grey skies blue.
It's raining,
And I always think of you:
Not because I'm sad,
But because I love you.

SHOOTING FOR THE MOON

09.12.2020

I want to write you a poem,
But I don't know what to say.
I feel like we've been really busy
These past few days.
I've been getting lost in planning
And all the busyness of life
When at the end of the day
All I want to do is hold you tight.
So yes,
Writing a poem
Is what I'm trying to do,
But all that comes to mind is,
"I so very much
Love and
Appreciate
Who you are
And all that you do."

SHOOTING FOR THE MOON

12.04.2020

I love the way you hold me tight
When we're snuggling on the couch at night.
You are precious to hold.
I love the way you hold me tight
And how our bodies curve together just right.
You are precious to kiss.
I love the way you hold me tight;
Being wrapped in your arms is pure bliss.
Your warmth and your body—it just feels so right.

SHOOTING FOR THE MOON

12.06.2021

I love the soft mornings
When I wake up slowly
And realize your side of the bed is cold,
Only to find you snuggled
On the couch with your laptop, or a book—
Looking at me over your glasses
With a cute smile that says
“That’s my wife” or
“She’s adorable,”
And we give soft morning kisses,
And soft hugs,
And the light filters through the window
Into my heart.
It filters through the window into my heart.

05.11.2022

The weight of a wife's prayer:
All evil beware.
No devil should dare
To go against the mighty
Weight of love
Stored within
The godly wife's prayer.

SHOOTING FOR THE MOON

05.04.2023

Wish we could go back
To when we were young and in love—
When we didn't have a care and
I could fall into your arms and be calm.
Because now when I hug you,
I feel the weight of the world on your shoulders.
I feel the stress on our minds when we kiss.
I wish time would slow down,
And I wish we could touch
Without feeling like life
Is busy—
Running around us
Never stopping.
But I'm glad we can't go back
Or else the weight on your shoulders
Wouldn't be evenly distributed to mine
When we hug.
Or else the stress in our minds
Wouldn't dissipate when we kiss.
Or else I wouldn't be reminded
As the busyness of life runs around us
To stop and feel everything with you—
To remember that time
Is precious and often short changed.
To stop and remember
That we are still young and in love,
And I can fall into your arms and be calm.

12.06.2023

The significance of this ring:
More than its status,
More than just bling,
A diamond reminder that our love
Is not a fragile thing.
More than its sparkle,
More than just shine,
A diamond reminder I'll always be yours
And you'll always be mine.

SHOOTING FOR THE MOON

03.24.2024

I miss you every Sunday
Since you've been away,
And there's something about
Sunsets that signal the sadness—
The sadness screaming in the
Dead silence of the apartment
So that I can hear my heartbeat.
Alone.
But every time my ring sparkles,
I'm reminded how much you
Light up my life,
So I hold on to the fact that
I know this silence
Will only last through the night,
And when the moon rises in the sky,
I smile and hold tight to the love
Our beating hearts hold inside.

SHOOTING FOR THE MOON

11.17.2025

We're living in the future—
You're by my side,
I'm by yours.
Look at who we've become:
Look at what we've accomplished.
Look at our love!
It wasn't hard to imagine.
This wasn't just a dream:
We've turned our hopes into reality.

SHOOTING FOR THE MOON

12.10.2025

One plus one equals two.
Mathematically that's the truth,
But one plus one can equal three
If you think about it biologically.
Three is a party;
Three is a crowd;
Three is a family:
A family which we made
And of which I could not be
More honored or proud.

SHOOTING FOR THE MOON

12.13.2025

Let’s play dominos
At nine at night
While the baby is asleep
And tucked in tight.
Kiss me on the nose
When the mood is right;
You’re winning by ten points—
Mischievous grin shining bright.

SHOOTING FOR THE MOON

12.15.2025

Seven years ago, I was shooting for the moon
To find that special somebody;
I hoped to find them soon.
To miss and land among the stars
Would have been okay too,
But I aim more accurately than I thought,
Or surely it was God who pointed the shot,
Because I hit the moon:
I landed you.

ACKNOWLEDGMENTS

Thank you to my amazing husband for allowing me to share our love story with the world through these poems. I thank God for giving me a beautiful love story and for continuing to write it.

Lastly, I would like to thank my husband again for bouncing the baby multiple times at night so that I could finish this book. Your patience, devotion, and encouragement never cease to amaze me.

ABOUT THE AUTHOR

D. Lisette believes that love stories can glorify God. She writes poetry about faith, love, and finding grace in everyday moments—from kitchen dances with her husband to bedtime prayers with her daughter.

A simple soul who delights in sunsets, good coffee, and the way love transforms ordinary days into something sacred, D. Lisette lives in Arizona where she also runs Luna Publishing LLC, helping indie authors bring their books to life.

This is her second poetry collection.

ALSO BY D. LISETTE

P(i)e(a)ce of My Mind: A Poem Book. A collection of honest poetry about battling depression, spiritual warfare, and discovering that you're never too broken for God's love.

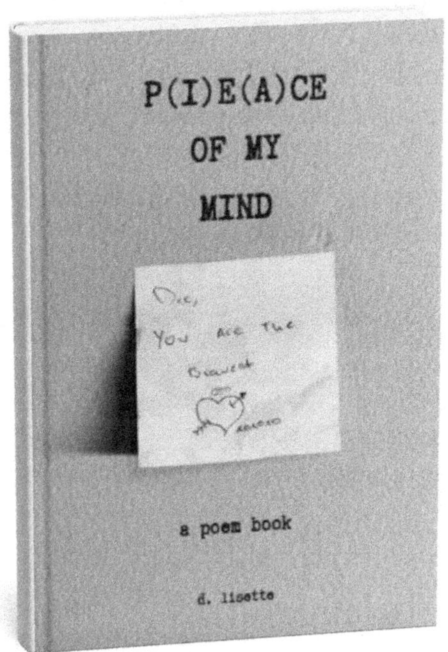

Available on Amazon.

THANK YOU FOR READING

Did you enjoy Shooting for the Moon?

Your review helps other readers discover this book, and it means more to me than you know.

If you purchased from or prefer a particular platform, please consider leaving a review there:

- Amazon Search "Shooting for the Moon D. Lisette," scroll to "Customer Reviews," and click "Write a customer review."
- Barnes & Noble Search "Shooting for the Moon D. Lisette," scroll to "Reviews," and click "Write a Review."
- Goodreads Search "Shooting for the Moon D. Lisette" and click "Write a Review."

Any platform, any words. An honest review makes a real difference.

Thank you for reading,
D. Lisette

www.ingramcontent.com/pod-product-compliance
Lightning Source LLC
LaVergne TN
LVHW020511100826
845148LV00003B/762

9798218933760